PRIMARY SOURCES OF AMERICAN WARS™

The War of 1812

Georgene Poulakidas

The Rosen Publishing Group's

PowerKids Press™
PRIMARY SOURCE

For my mother and father

Published in 2006 by The Rosen Publishing Group, Inc.
29 East 21st Street, New York, NY 10010

Copyright © 2006 by The Rosen Publishing Group, Inc.

First Edition

Editor: Eric Fein
Book Design: Erica Clendening
Photo Researcher: Adriana Skura

Photo Credits: Cover image and pp. 8, 14, 18, 20 (inset) © Clements Library, University of Michigan; p. 4 Courtesy of Historical Society of Pennsylvania Collection/ Bridgeman Art Library, (inset) National Archives and Records Administration; p. 8 (inset) © Francis G. Mayer/Corbis; pp. 10, 18 (inset), 20 New York Historical Society, New York/Bridgeman Art Library, (inset) Atwater Kent Museum of Philadelphia/Bridgeman Art Library; p. 12 © Burstein Collection/Corbis, (inset) © Hulton/Archive/Getty Images; p. 14 (inset) Library of Congress, Map Division; p. 16 Library of Congress, Washington D.C./Bridgeman Art Library, (inset) © Bettmann/Corbis.

Library of Congress Cataloging-in-Publication Data

Poulakidas, Georgene.
    The War of 1812 / Georgene Poulakidas.—1st ed.
    p. cm. — (Primary sources of American wars)
    Includes bibliographical references (p.) and index.
    Contents: An uneasy peace — The impressment of American sailors—Caught in the
    middle —Conflict with Native Americans — The war begins — Americans attack British
    Canada —British attack the American east coast —The Battle of New Orleans —The war ends.
    ISBN 1-4042-2681-8 (lib. bdg.)
    1. United States—History—War of 1812—Juvenile literature. [1. United
    States—History—War of 1812.] I. Title. II. Series.

    E354.P68 2006
    973.5'2—dc22
                                                    2003022414

Manufactured in the United States of America

Contents

The American Revolutionary War ended with the signing of the Treaty of Paris (left). This page from the treaty shows the signatures of some of the officials who signed it, including Americans John Adams and Benjamin Franklin.

An Uneasy Peace

From 1775 to 1783, the American **colonies** fought the **American Revolutionary War** against England. After winning the war, the colonies established themselves as the United States of America. Though the fighting had ended, problems remained between England and the United States. These problems would grow worse and become the causes of the War of 1812.

Many historians believe there were three main causes of the war. The first was the **impressment**, or taking by force, of American sailors by the British navy. Another cause was England's attempts to stop Americans from trading in Europe and from expanding further west in North America. A third cause was the belief that the British were urging Native Americans to attack American frontier **settlements**.

■ *The Battle of Princeton (left) was fought on January 3, 1777. By winning this important battle, American colonists felt assured they could win the American Revolutionary War.*

In June 1813, Chesapeake *lost a sea battle to the British ship*, Shannon. *Chesapeake's captain, James Lawrence, died during the battle. His dying words, "Don't give up the ship!" become a call to arms to American soldiers and sailors during the War of 1812.*

The Impressment of American Sailors

The life of a British sailor was a difficult one. Many British sailors left their ships and joined the crews of American ships, where they were paid more and had better living conditions. British ships then began to stop American ships and search them for British sailors. However, between 1803 and 1810, about 5,000 American citizens were impressed to serve on British ships. The most serious act of impressment happened in June 1807. The British warship *Leopard* opened fire on the American warship *Chesapeake*. Three Americans were killed and 18 others were hurt. Four men from the *Chesapeake* were accused of being British deserters and were killed by the British. It was later learned that three of these men were American citizens. This act of violence against the American ship became known as the Chesapeake Affair.

■ *This picture shows British sailors attacking the crew of* Chesapeake. *The picture was printed in London, England, in 1816.*

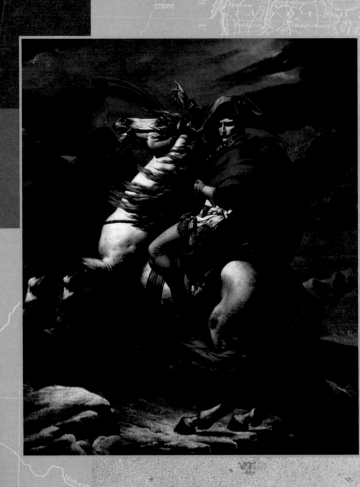

Napoleon Bonaparte was ruler of France from 1804 to 1814. Among his accomplishments was organizing a set of French laws called the Napoleonic Code. The laws addressed civil rights, property ownership, and contracts.

Caught in the Middle

From the late 1700s to the early 1800s, France and England fought a war. France's leader, Napoleon Bonaparte, wanted to gain control of Europe. At the time, both countries traded with the United States. However, each nation wanted to stop the other from trading with the Americans. Between 1803 and 1812, England and France seized about 1,500 U.S. ships on the seas.

In 1807, the U.S. **Congress** passed a law that stopped Americans from trading with other countries. The U.S. government hoped that this would stop England and France from taking more of its ships. However, it did not. American businesses were hurt by the law. In 1809, another law was passed. This law allowed the United States to trade with other countries, but not England and France. However, U.S. ships continued to be taken by England and France.

■ *In the years before the war, the British navy tried to keep U.S. ships from moving freely. Once the war started, England sent about 100 ships to America to block the movement of U.S. ships. This 1813 painting shows British navy ships off the coast of New England.*

William Henry Harrison became the ninth president of the United States. He died only a month after taking office.

Conflict with Native Americans

As white settlers moved westward across America, disagreements with Native Americans became common. Native Americans were angry because they were being forced from their lands. Fighting often broke out.

By 1811, a Native American named Tecumseh and his brother Tenskwatawa, put together a union of several thousand Native Americans to fight off the white settlers in the Indiana territory, near Canada. The governor of this **territory**, William Henry Harrison, led a group of about 1,000 U.S. soldiers in a battle against the Native Americans near the Tippecanoe River in Indiana. The soldiers won the battle but found British guns and gunpowder among the belongings of the Native Americans.

Many Americans came to believe that the British had to be stopped from supplying **weapons** to the Native Americans.

■ *This battle (left) between American forces and Native Americans took place at the Tippecanoe River. During the fighting, the American forces destroyed the Native Americans' village.*

Henry Clay (left) was one of the U.S. congressmen known as the War Hawks. Some War Hawks also wanted to take Canada away from the British, who controlled the country. Clay helped draw up the terms for the treaty that ended the War of 1812.

The War Begins

As problems with England continued, a group of congressmen from the western and southern states pushed for America to go to war with the British. They were called the War Hawks. They believed the United States needed to protect its trade interests and its settlers.

On June 18, 1812, President James Madison finally asked the U.S. Congress to **declare**, or announce, war against England. Two days before the United States went to war, the British government decided to stop the impressment of American sailors. However, there was no way to get news of their decision to the United States in time.

The United States soon discovered that it was not well prepared for war. The U.S. Army was made up of less than 10,000 men. Most of them had never before fought in a battle.

■ *James Madison (left) was the fourth president of the United States. He served from 1809 to 1817.*

This map shows some of the areas in the United States and Canada where the War of 1812 was fought. The map was printed in a book in 1813.

14

Americans Attack British Canada

In 1812, the United States attacked British forces in Canada from three different locations. The United States attacked near Niagara Falls, New York; Detroit, Michigan; and the north shore of Lake Champlain. All three attacks failed, causing the Americans to suffer many losses.

In September 1813, Oliver Hazard Perry won control of Lake Erie as the U.S. Navy defeated a British fleet of ships. Perry had been put in control of the U.S. Navy ships in Lake Erie. On October 5, 1813, U.S. forces were also successful in the Battle of the Thames River in Canada. This battle was fought against the British and the Native Americans who had joined forces with the British Canadians. Tecumseh was killed during the battle.

■ *This picture shows Oliver Hazard Perry during the naval battle for Lake Erie. Perry's father was a naval officer too. Perry joined the U.S. Navy when he was about 14 years old and served on his father's ship, the* General Greene.

Francis Scott Key (at left, with his hand out toward the flag) wrote a poem after seeing the attack on Fort McHenry. The American flag that flew over the fort during the battle is now on display in the National Museum of American History in Washington, D.C.

16

British Attack the American East Coast

On August 18, 1814, the British landed about 3,500 troops in Maryland. These troops set out for Washington, D.C. On August 24, they attacked the city. The British set fire to the White House, the U.S. Capitol, the navy yard, and several other buildings.

On September 13, the British attacked **Fort** McHenry, in the harbor of Baltimore, Maryland. The attack on the fort was witnessed by an American lawyer, Francis Scott Key. American forces held off the attack. Key was inspired to write a poem about the battle. The poem was turned into a song, "The Star-Spangled Banner."

By the end of the summer, both the United States and England had become tired of the fighting. Peace talks began in Ghent, Belgium.

■ *When British forces reached Washington, D.C., they found that the president and most government officials had escaped. While there, the British destroyed many important U.S. government buildings.*

Andrew Jackson's success at the Battle of New Orleans made him a war hero and very popular with the people. He became the seventh president of the United States (1829–1837).

The Battle of New Orleans

On December 24, 1814, the United States and Great Britain signed the Treaty of Ghent. The **treaty** ended the war. However, the fighting did not stop because news of the signing traveled slowly.

On January 8, 1815, a British army of about 7,500 men attacked New Orleans, Louisiana. General Andrew Jackson led about 5,000 American troops. Jackson also had the help of Jean and Pierre Lafitte, who were leaders of a **pirate** group from the Louisiana waters. American troops easily defeated the British army.

The fighting between British and American troops in the Battle of New Orleans lasted for only a day. However, it was the final battle of the war.

■ *The Battle of New Orleans (left) was one of England's worst military defeats. About 2,000 British soldiers died in the battle, compared to a loss of about 70 American soldiers.*

The Treaty of Ghent (left) officially ended the War of 1812. John Quincy Adams and Henry Clay were among the U.S. officials who signed this treaty.

The War Ends

On February 17, 1815, Congress approved the Treaty of Ghent. The war with England was finally over. Yet neither the United States or England gained much. Both sides were returned land that had been taken by the other during the war. The treaty did not even address the impressment of U.S. sailors. Some people call the War of 1812, "the war nobody won."

However, Native Americans did not fare well, losing the support of the British. American settlers then forced Native Americans from their lands in the Northwest and the South.

The United States gained **international** respect following the war. It was now seen as a nation that would defend its interests at any cost. The young nation had become an important world power.

■ *To honor the United States' victory in the War of 1812, special handkerchiefs were made (left). These handkerchiefs showed scenes of the battles that America had won during the war.*

Timeline

1775–1783	The American Revolutionary War is fought.
Early 1800s	England and France fight a war.
1807	The British warship *Leopard* attacks the American warship *Chesapeake*.
1807	The U.S. Congress passes a law to stop Americans from trading with other countries.
1809	The U.S. Congress passes a law that allows Americans to again trade with other countries, except England and France.
1811	The Battle of Tippecanoe is fought between the U.S. and Native Americans.
June 18, 1812	U.S. Congress declares war against England.
1812	Americans attack British forces in Canada.
September 1813	Oliver Hazard Perry wins control of Lake Erie. The U.S. Navy defeats a fleet of British ships.
October 5, 1813	U.S. forces win the Battle of the Thames River in Canada.
August 24, 1814	British forces attack Washington, D.C.
September 13, 1814	British naval forces attack Fort McHenry in Maryland.
December 24, 1814	The United States and England sign the Treaty of Ghent.
January 8, 1815	The United States wins the Battle of New Orleans, the final battle of the War of 1812.
February 17, 1815	The U.S. Congress officially approves the Treaty of

Glossary

American Revolutionary War (uh-MER-uh-kuhn rev-uh-LOO-shuh-ner-ee WOR) The war from 1775–1783 during which the American colonies fought against England. As a result, the United States of America was created.

colonies (KOL-uh-neez) Territories that have been settled by people from another country and are controlled by that country.

Congress (KONG-griss) The government body of the United States that makes laws, made up of the Senate and the House of Representatives.

declare (di-KLAIR) To announce something formally.

fort (FORT) A building that is strongly built to survive attacks.

impressment (im-PRESS-muhnt) To force a person to work against his or her will.

international (in-tur-NASH-uh-nuhl) Involving different countries.

pirate (PYE-rit) Someone who attacks and steals from ships at sea.

settlements (SET-uhl-muhnts) Colonies or groups of people who have left one place to make a home in another.

territory (TER-uh-tor-ee) The land and waters under the control of a state, nation, or ruler.

treaty (TREE-tee) A formal agreement between two or more countries.

weapons (WEP-uhnz) Things that can be used in a fight to attack or defend, such as swords, guns, knives, or bombs.

Index

Primary Sources

Cover: The U.S.S. *Chesapeake* under attack by H.M.S. Shannon [c. 1800s]. One of four prints of the battle by J.C. Schetky. **Page 4 (inset):** The Treaty of Paris [1783]. National Archives. **Page 4:** *Battle of Princeton on 3rd January 1777*. [Date Unknown]. Oil on canvas by William Mercer. Atwater Kent Museum of Philadelphia. **Page 6 (inset):** The USS *Chesapeake* battling the HMS *Shannon* [1816]. Created by Tanners J. Webster. Clement's Library at the University of Michigan. **Page 6:** The Boarding and Taking of the American Ship *Chesapeake* [1816]. Clement's Library at the University of Michigan. **Page 8 (inset):** *Napoleon on Horseback at the St. Bernard Pass* [1801]. Painted by Jacques-Louis David. **Page 8:** *Blockade of New England* [1813]. Watercolor painting by William Paine. Clement's Library at the University of Michigan. **Page 10 (inset):** *William Henry Harrison* [c. Nineteenth Century]. Oil on canvas by Bass Otis. Atwater Kent Museum of Philadelphia. **Page 10:** Attack of the Native Americans at the Tippecanoe River, Indiana Territory, 7th November 1811 [c. Nineteenth Century]. Color lithograph. Artist Unknown. New York Historical Society. **Page 12 (inset):** Henry Clay [c. 1850]. **Page 12:** *James Madison* [c. 1805]. Oil on canvas by Gilbert Stuart. **Page 14 (inset):** A Correct Map of the Seat of War [1813]. Published in a book by Samuel Lewis. Library of Congress. **Page 14:** *Perry's Victory on Lake Erie* [1815]. Painting. Artist Unknown. Clement's Library at the University of Michigan. **Page 16 (inset):** Francis Scott Key observing Fort McHenry from aboard ship [c. Nineteenth Century]. Artist Unknown. **Page 16:** Representation of the Capture of the City of Washington by the British forces, August 24th 1814, from 'The Stationer's Almanack' [c. 1815]. Engraving. Artist Unknown. Library of Congress. **Page 18 (inset):** *Andrew Jackson* [1835]. Oil on canvas by Asher Brown Durand. New-York Historical Society. **Page 18:** *Battle of New Orleans* [1816]. Drawn by E. Seymour and engraved by J. W. Steel. Clement's Library at the University of Michigan. **Page 20 (inset):** The final page of the Treaty of Ghent [1814]. Clement's Library at the University of Michigan. **Page 20:** Kerchief commemorating the victories of the War of 1812 [c. 1815]. New York Historical Society.

Web Sites

Due to the changing nature of Internet links, PowerKids Press has developed an online list of Web sites related to the topic of this book. This site is updated regularly. Please use this link to access the list:
http://www.powerkidslinks.com/psaw/w12/